VOLUME
BOOK OF
LIVED

Penny Authors

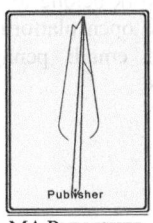

MA PUBLISHER

Penny Authors

Copyright © Mayar Akash 2018

Produced by Penny Authors
Published by MA Publishing
First published July 2018

ISBN-13: 9781910499351

All rights reserved. No part of this publication may be reproduced, stored in a retrieval system, or transmitted, in any form or by any means, electronic, mechanical, photocopying, recording, public performances or otherwise, without prior written permission of the copyright holder, except for brief quotations embodied in critical articles or reviews.

Disclaimer:

All expressions and opinions of the work belong to the artists and PA does not share or endorse any other than to provide the open platform to publish their work. For further information on PA policies please email: pennyauthors@yahoo.co.uk for further information and submission guidelines.

Cover designed by Mayar Akash
Cover photo by Mayar Akash
Typeset in Times Roman

CONTENT

Introduction	7
Beautiful Mind	9
Nighs In Life	10
Last To Know	11
Me And Myself	12
Planned	13
Living	14
Don't Hold Back	16
Cover Up's	17
Inner Peace	18
Aliens	19
Happiness	20
Empty Thoughts	21
Beauty	22
Playing The Game	23
Back Burner	24
The Tyranny Of 2017	25
What You Lost	26
16	27
Deep Water	28
The Winter That Shapes Me...(Sylheti)	29
Don't Grow Up	30
Love Demon	31
Ordinary	32
Tell Them	33
Earth Father (For My Beautiful Dad - Rip)	34
Sickness	35
Session	36
Kiss The Pain	37
People	38
Spirit Of Discontent	39
Duhk, Suhk	40
Who Comes First	41
Without You	42
Romance	43
Brothers And Sisters	44
Silent Thoughts	45
Standing In The Middle	46
Adversity	47

Unleash My Pain	48
Squeeze Me	49
Seize It	50
On Your Own	51
The Dew Of Meteorology	52
By Nirmal Kaur	52
Dark Room	53
Bad Byes	54
On Air	55
Fixated	56
A Droplet Amongst Thousands	57
What Is Your Colour?	58
Ripple	59
Deshi Girl	60
In Life	61
My Little Soul	62
Believe	63
Shoes	64
My Side Of The Story	65
Corners Of My Mind	67
The Daffodil	68
If Love Means	69
Novelty-Ness	70
Let Go	71
Princess Diana	72
Believing	73
Use To Think	74
My Bewildered Mind	75
Upbringing	76
Freedom	77
Glastonbury Chalice	78
The Weight Of Your Stare	79
Heart Watering	80
Hold Your Tears	81
Grow Out Of Your Childhood	82
Being Strong Enough	83
On Top Of Me	84
Why Special Then	85
Conmen's Victims	86
Point In Life	87
Branded By A Kick	88
Who Are You To Judge	89

Man And Woman	90
Nature	91
Eat My Words	92
Steps Of Blood	93
Gorgeous Girl	94
Bus Job	95
Frack E.U	96
Your Stare	97
One Of My Wonders	98
Tell A Lie	99
Can't Forget The Weight	100
Mourn	101
Fruits Of Independence	102
Re-Gain	103
My April Love	104
My Valentine	105
Identity	106
Out Of Touch	107
Soul Cry	108
Windmills	109
Witch Love	110
Photo Gallery	111

Penny Authors

Introduction

Welcome to the fourth accomplishment of the Penny Authors' Anthology. The previous three anthologies have been a success and as a result we have attracted new poets in this editions.

We at Penny Authors like to recognise, remind and remember all the Penny Authors that have taken part past always and present:

1. Zainab Khan,
2. Paul Harvey,
3. Isaac Harvey,
4. Rebekah Vaughan,
5. Rabia Mehmood,
6. Tamanna Parveen,
7. Ellis Dixon-King,
8. Liam Newton,
9. Professor Muhammad Nurul Huque,
10. Kalam Choudhury,
11. Rashma Mehta,
12. Mathew Whiting
13. Akik Miah
14. NirmalKaur
15. Mayar Akash
16. Julie Archbold
17. Lora Ashman

The experiences that is captured in the anthology are colourful and the times that they've happened give it the flavour. PA wants to bring to the world, the world within and show the abundances to our lives. We all ride "the ride of life" from different points but all travel to the heart/centre of what life is.

In this book you will feel and experience journeys that will take you in and out, emotional, mentally and spiritually. Let yourself get on a ride that will become a merry-go-round then may turn to a roller coaster, it will take you through life of all ages and some familiar experiences and occurrences, to some out of this world or weird and wonderful.

This is the fourth book of lived, that lets you live life along with yours. If you would like to get involved then email pennyauthors@yahoo.co.uk.

So see you on the other side email us on pennyauthors@yahoo.co.uk.

Finally, we hope you will enjoy reading the Book of Lived.

Beautiful Mind
by Tamanna Parvin

I watched from the tallest tower as you lay there.
The tears trickling down your cheek.
I tried to resuscitate you.
Forgive me.
The walls closed in,
As I looked at you.
Everything around me drifted.
Falling into the deepest of oceans.
I was never a good swimmer.
They didn't change in eighty years,
but their skin wrinkled like snowflakes.
Tell me will I live?
I want to paint you a picture,
so let my words make you wonder.
Intrigued as you may be,
Me and you were not alike.

Nighs In Life
by Mayar Akash

Changes in life the way you see it, thus
not the way you know it
despite the anger and frustration
the poverty of thoughts
nighs the past in debt to the future; leaves a scar
Changes in life the way it found you.

Times that changes thus the minutes
still stay the same time that silently whisper the day and
silently blink the night away.

Changes in time, illusions the mind
deprives the soul and numbs the body
time the forceless reality
beholds the demand less ventures into time
begetting the existence.

Last To Know
by Mayar Akash

Happy news, sad news
for me it's always the last news.

Rays of sunshine and grey clouds I see
as I stand proud

Yet mute and faint to be in presence
with the news that revolves around me.

Far from near, words get around
round to my silence to stretch my sounds.

End is where I'm best at home
when life is complete.

Me And Myself
by Mayar Akash

My time has come to feel alone
days seem so far away
nights feel eternity away
my heart stopped again
I know I'm slipping away
can't stop or wait
I know I'll be late to face my fate.

My love has gone
my feelings whispered away
my mind has rested aside
my joy seems to be far from me
nor here or anywhere.

My life has shadowed its days
my soul has witnessed them pay
my beliefs have swam
in the air current that passed my way
My body my flesh and blood
agonised the suffering
taunted me and myself.

Planned
by Mayar Akash

I thought I had it planned
in my head
on how to live my life

To have security,
love,
kindness
warmth,
to achieve goals set to keep us
comfortable in our later life

To respect and be equal
to each other and share responsibilities.
Can't handle it anymore.

Living
by Liam Newton

Every day I think of the life I'm living
fuck sake feels like I'm in prison
snakes hissing cameras clicking
fucked system we live in
roll safe god willing
mad music man
it's hard to make a killing
slowly ill make a living
off my batch of lyrics
that I'm spitting
it's sickening
are you listening
get rid of him
I aint mimicking
streets killing him
he's missing
he's wishing
I'm living
he's sinning

spitting lyrical incisions
I aint mimicking trap life
that's just sickening
I'm on it
are you listening
he aint a big boy
get rid of him
the streets are killing him
he aint about that life
pick up that pen
fuck the knife
words are weapons
aim down your sight

Cont.

onto that paper
you aint out here just to be a money maker
you aint got be balling like a laker
god forsake us
if he's there
would he let us buss
buss shots
at those lives we choose to corrupt
fly like doves
freedom is a must
look at them just mugs
filled up with rage and locked on like cuffs
there on stuff
were on stuff
in their pockets
they've got drugs stuffed
for personal uses or to f**k up other recluses
this system is useless

what is life?

this is life!

Don't Hold Back
by Mayar Akash

When you love somebody
and you want more
You know that and so do they
and they want you too

So don't hold back
get straight to the point
don't mess about
don't fool around
don't hide your feelings
say it out loud to them.

Remember this
you'll have to compromise
and don't settle for less
it's not worth the stress
so don't hold back.

Cover Up's
by Mayar Akash

When respect you lose
and nationals despise

when you've entered sin
and its coloured you bad

when you get renown for your deeds
and reputation you cannot abort.

there's only one way out
and that's to cover up

cover up and hide
hide yourself in Islam

hide your deeds under the hijab
hide your sin amongst the Muslims.

Inner Peace
by Mayar Akash

Can't seem to find my inner peace
but I have everything in place

Can't seem to find my way
but there's no dead ends

Can't seem to see clear ahead
but there's nothing to hold me back

Can't seem to find my inner peace
I'm lost inside
I've been there before
but times have changed and
I've been finding it hard

I'm going round and round in circles
I'm in a maze without
a way out.

Aliens
by Mayar Akash

We search and we research
we gaze and we stare
looking to find something
or someone we don't know of

we don't know what it or
how they look like, we only perceive what Mr. Spielberg
conceived

We look far and away but never at us or within
we've ventured out in space, but never deep within

If we look deep enough and understand what we do
I don't think we'll be far from an alien within us.

In every one of us there's an alien within

How can an alien b what we perceive
how can an alien be human
like that what we all imagine

we're all made to believe that there is
a parallel world in another dimension
so be it and only there
that's where you'll find some like me.

Happiness
by Rashma Mehta

Happiness is believing
Happiness is reality
Happiness is different
Happiness is real

Happiness is laughter
Happiness is proven
Happiness is joy
Happiness can happen

Happiness is driven
Happiness is focus
Happiness is true
Happiness is dreaming

Empty Thoughts
by Mayar Akash

Sun rises the day begins
My heart aches my heart breaks
Can't throw them away
can't stop them from coming my way
can't loosen my mind
don't know how to
don't know who to
Show what happens inside

Can't release the force, pressure that builds

The agony that hits, my heart takes the beats
My mind loses its senses, the reason is you

You who give me life
you who make me feel someone
You who make me mean someone
where there is nothing, darkness
darkness as you sleep
emptiness that lives
nothing left in sight
darkness leads to you
the thoughts of you spill in
lighting the darkness
filling the emptiness
Thus my heart dampens
knowing you
is nothing more than an empty thoughts.

Beauty
by Mayar Akash

Oh beauteous of beauty
come tell me your secret
what is your morals to beauty
Tell me oh tell me and look at me
tell me am I so fine
am I beautiful tell me oh please tell me

Have I got pimples
have I got moles
and have I got various spots
and acnes of various sizes

I can't face it while you make it
I feel embarrassed while you have fun
I hide my face when you come by.

The beauty lies in the bread winner
oh beauteous of beauty
you have yours and I have mine
so use it wisely
don't waste it and make others unhappy

In the end it will cost you
it does not stay forever
There are other waiting in the future
so beauteous of beauty
come pass it on don't be hasty
while you could be having fun
so share your beauty's secret and take care
oh beauteous of beauty.

Playing The Game
by Mayar Akash

There was a time when you looked into my eyes and said,
"true love is greater than ever".
That time I felt my mind unloading the doubts and thoughts
the world had just begun.
No sooner than done the problems had begun,
after all that love and affection that I gave and trouble I bared.
The sacrifice I took, giving my heart and mind the pits.
Now it seems like you played a game and I played the fool.
Now you're going away and I'm here left on my own with bitter acidic
feelings.

Tell me now who do I turn to with these bitter feelings that i have
No one but a distinct shadow when the sun goes down and the moon
comes up
the shadows of you fade.
The thought of you leaving squeezes my heart to tears
the price i pay for being a fool.
Yet no one can create the same moments we had created.
The history we made where memories still linger where the heartaches
haunt to seek refuge and take revenge.

While my heart weeps and my mind builds on its sites of being a fool
the time and strategy taken
The record we kept, the experience we touched, the beauty of you and the
sheer desire in me has led to this.
My feelings regret the loss of you and most of all me being alive when
you're not around

I feel it pounding so strongly that my heart is weakening
I feel like killing where as I am dying
as I'll take the thoughts of you till the day I die
to leave this world in peace to rest
for this is the result of playing the game.

Back Burner
by Mayar Akash

While you study…
do what I wanted to do
I take the back seat

A part of my life has stopped
it's hurting bad
its starving my mind

My hearts giving me pain
while I baby sit
waiting for you.

For you
my life is on the back burner.

The Tyranny of 2017
by Nirmal Kaur

The end of the tumultuous tyranny
of profit and Selby.
The analysis of truth verses.
Disorder = allowed to be personal
for the greater good of what's personally important to me.
Me alone
as I am without partner
and ridiculously a good survivor
from the wrath of the swot team.
1 down,
three to go
the positioning of the power of two still around.

However W the power of 50/50
is the blatancy of a militant struggle
that's never ending to me.
Was over the moon too
knew that Annie's Pantry forgave me
was a little offshore with my sight.

What You Lost
by Mayar Akash

You don't know
what you had

until you lose
all that you had

you only know
what you had

when you lose
everything

You don't know what you lost
until you lose it.

16
by Mayar Akash

Tender 16
warm 16
lovely 16
happy 16
rosy 16
sweet 16
sugar 16
candy 16
love 16
honey 16
kiss 16
good old 16

Deep Water
by Mayar Akash

When I'm around you
I'm in deep water

This is when I get the feeling
I've jumped in the deep end

my love for you drowns me
as it flows over back to me

I know what I have done
but I can only go so far

I know I'm taking a chance
but it's a chance I got to take

Everything is above my head
but I drown with the love I have for you.

The Winter That Shapes Me...(Sylheti)
by Akik Miah

Ghor tanda ammee tanda	(The house is cold and I am cold)
Bar rah and-dyer	(outside its dark)
Arr bat-tash barah tanda	(and the wind outside is cold)
Gas ah-stay ah-stay	(trees slowly slowly)
More reeeeea zzzzhar	(DDDDYYYYiiinnnngggg) dying.
Be yan ammee tanda	(It's the morning and I am cold)
ammee utt yah kammo zhai	(I get up and go to work)
Tobo ammee tanda	(I am still cold)
Arr aahsta deen and-dyer bar rah	(All day its dark outside all day)
ammee Fat tore lack khan tanda.	(I am cold like a stone)
Kam shesh Ghor-raw zai yah	(I finish work and go home)
Tobo barah and-dyer	(and still outside its still dark)
Be-annay tanda bikal tanda.	(Morning it's cold and evening it's cold)
Shan-tee faye nah tanda taki	(I can't find peace from this cold)
Shesh kun-deen shesh oi bo kun din	(when will this end when will this finish.)
Forty din	(everyday)
Shoman	(The same)
Shoman	(The same)
Shoman	(The same)
Ammee beshi bezar	(I am very sad)
Pause	
Ahck-tah bod lah	(a sudden change)
Foo roo bat tea	(There's a small light)
Ammee sai Arr raw	(I want more and more)
Arr raw	
Ammee deck key Arr raw	(I can see more and more)
Arr raw Arr raw arraw	(I want more and more)
Roid, roid gorom roid	(Sun Sun warm Sun)
Ammee gor rom	(I am warm)
Ammee kushi bitho rare	(I am happy inside)
Fat toror lack khan tanda nai on nay.	(I am not cold like the stone anymore)
Ammee nor-rom on nai.	(I have become soft)
Gas zee-tah on nay fool eye say.. fruit.)	(The trees are alive and there is
Arr raw roid ammee on nai man nush	(There is more of the sun and now I become human)

Don't Grow Up
by Mayar Akash

Don't grow up
don't grow too fast
my little one

take your time
be a little child and a little kid
you'll only be a kid short while
and grow up to be old for a long while

Don't rush
don't plunder
don't grow up to quick,

Love Demon
by Mayar Akash

Oh love demon you've captured my heart
It's burning burning with desire only for you
You opened my heart and train my blood my love is not for
you my lady.

You mean nothing to me except evil deeds
What love means to me can never describe you.
I can feel the loves heat getting hotter and hotter
I feel it on my body and on my lips.

You've captured my heart you've tortured my mind
Your love means nothing to me, my hatred and your desire for
my love is getting at its highest.
Your love is burning its worth nothing just trouble.

You melt your beauty in my eyes I fall a pray to you
you captured my heart but your evil shields me from your love.
For you can never capture my love, but oh love demon
your love must be great and your beauty's full of grace yet
your nature throws it away in disgrace.

You become lost in your words and in your own fear
your hearts begins to hurt, You burst in tears you drown your
evil fire
You free yourself, free from the evil, the evil that seeks for evil.

You try to act innocent but the evil still lingers in you
Its hard to act kind and gentle
you try to stay away from love and try to for
get everything and start all over again.

Ordinary
by Mayar Akash

You are no one special
you are just ordinary
you are common
common as everyone

You are no extra ordinary
you are just ordinary
you are same
same as everybody

You are no one uncommon
you are just common
common as far as the eyes can see
you just same as the rest.

Tell Them
by Mayar Akash

Don't hold back
tell them your feelings
tell them your expectation
tell them your needs
tell them your desires
tell them your fantasies
tell them your dreams
tell them your future

But don't tell them your secrets
don't tell them your past
don't tell them your pains
don't tell them your sins
don't tell them your disappointments
don't tell them your how many friends you had
it's not the time to…

tell them you love her
tell them you want her
tell them you want more
tell them when you accept me
There's more.

Earth Father (for my beautiful Dad - RIP)
by Julie Archbold

Earth father, bringer of life
Neglected in your strife
Our mother, your wife

Have your sons lost their way
To dream of another day
Where the sins of the world must pay

Earth Father, make rise your name
So that humble souls may rue the game
And neither gender take the blame

We are here now, your children
And will never be balanced without your love
When our Mother cries over your oppression
We need you to light our way

Many siblings have forgotten
Resisting inner strength and outer fortitude
Of nimble body and heart full of passion
For that planet upon which we stand

How this must sadden My Father
Seer of the paradox
Who lives simply to please, with ease
Who is quiet and at peace with his nature

I see you Father
And I wish to resurrect the respect
Of which you are assured
From me

Sickness
by Mayar Akash

We have all been there &
for those who have not
you will be there too

Love and hunger, deaf and blind
there is no room
for anyone else.

We forget everything &
we lash out to everyone closest
so much so that we throw away everything
only to settle for one.

Everyone gets there
once your there
it is a place
you will always
find in times of loneliness.

Session
by Mayar Akash

It happens to all of us
love creeps up and obsession breaks us

We all go mad
everything we
touch goes sad

Obsession roots
depression shoots

When fruits of our desires
don't get the chance to roost

It happens to all of us
we fall a pray to a vicious cycle

of intense desire to have
have the things all made up

in the obsessed mind
and not in the heart of the one you desire.

Kiss The Pain
by Mayar Akash

I love you so much; and you've also hurt me as much
I've been around you for so long; that I can't imagine to live
without you
You made me cry so many times; you've given me pain and
now
I can't bear it anymore; no more ever again
You got a choice and I'm; giving you a last chance

So kiss my pain
kiss the pain away
and I mean kiss the pain

kiss the pain kiss it away
kiss the pain, kiss the pain

You've done me wrong; when all I did; was love you
So kiss my pain
kiss the pain away
and I mean kiss the pain

kiss the pain kiss it away
kiss the pain, kiss the pain

You have a last chance; if you want me; kiss my pain good bye
So kiss my pain
kiss the pain away
and I mean kiss the pain

kiss the pain kiss it away
kiss the pain, kiss the pain

People
by Mayar Akash

There's nice people
there's sinister people
there's bad people
there's evil people
there's clumsy people
there's mad people
there's polite people
there's rude people
there's charming people
there's uptight people
there's lost people
there's found people
there's people who use
there's people who get used
and there's me
1 in a million, billion, trillion
an angel in devils disguise.

Spirit Of Discontent
by Julie Archbold

Oh spirit of discontent
Take your snivelling carcass elsewhere

I beseech you
Give me my freedom
Unbind these rusted shackles

Why, I demand
Have I been sentenced thus?

Duhk, Suhk
by Mayar Akash

Hamara dil	(Our heart
Hamara jaan ek se hothi	our life is with one
tisree se nahin	not with third
Hazaro kha shohk hain	thousand have wish
ek se milthi hai	one receives
O hain mera zindegi	that's my life
Somaage giya tho ek	thought about the one
dusree kha bhat koi nahin	no need to talk about a second
Sochraa hain tho	thinking about it
pyar milthi tho nahin	yet can't find love
Dunya meh duhk	world has pain
dunya meh suhk	world has pleasure
uppaar seh tasveer	above a picture
neeche seh assue	below tears
Hamara jaan ek rasta meh giya	my life has traveled one road
suhkeh duhkeh muhabbat jathi	pleasure pain in love
pyar ka suhk kobi nahin milthi	there is never pleasure in love
Hazaro bhar aako meh assue athi	thousand time tears in eyes come
tho duhk nahin jaathi	but the pain doesn't go
pyar ka nishani	loves obsession
Saarah zindegi ek din jodi athi	if whole life came in a day
tho duhk nahin miltha tha	there would be no pain
Jo ouse din miltha tha tho	if that day was to come
muhabbat ka duhk suhk	loves pleasure and pain
hamara pass nahin atha tha.	would never come to us.)

Who Comes First
by Mayar Akash

People come first
babies come first
Infants come first
children come first
young people come first
invalid come first
disadvantage and deprived come first

Without You
by Rashma Mehta

Without you I feel lost
Without you I feel alone
Without you I feel empty
Without you I don't know how to be

Without you I feel lonely
Without you I feel like giving up
Without you I will never be me
Without you I don't know if I can continue

Without you I've struggled
Without you I've done my best
Without you I've messed up
Without you I've come out smiling
Without you I hope you're proud of me
Without you I don't know where I'd be
Without you I've come out stronger
Without you I've come out fighting
Without you I've got back on track

Romance
by Mayar Akash

Romance oh sweet romance
our sweet tender love is growing
let's romance let's make love in the candle light
Romance, romance up in the mountains
romance in sweet dreams.

Romance oh sweet romance
Table for two candles are lit romance is in the air
with an warm atmosphere
and the magic is in the air so let's romance

The touch of your lips make my pulse react
it's physical and it's logical
In the shadows we sit arms around us and with the sun setting
behind us the warm air indulging the moments we create.

We are romancing when our heart is relaxing
and our mind is enjoying and forget the world outside
When you look in my eyes
you turn me inside out
you show me what life was all about

Only you, the only one who stole my heart away
in my life there is no other love
your the only girl that my heart and soul would love.

So let's romance, romance together
in your eyes I could see them
twinkling so let's romance
let's make love
share it more with each other than throw it away.

Brothers And Sisters
by Mayar Akash

Sisters of beauty, brothers in love
let's get together and do the part
take a part in love
play the game
see it feel it and know it
what love really is
and to be free where love is not in a conflict.

Brothers and sisters, follow the instruction
and the guidance to love and take care
see how it goes.
Try to break through with each other
be strong and stand up together
and don't grow doubts in your thoughts
and start to show fear in your eyes emerge in tears
don't cover your mind with dullness and clouds with anger
where foolish things now conquer.

Brothers and sisters
has this world got any meaning and longer
Brothers and sisters, love don't last
love won't stay
Gives a lot of heartaches, and won't go away
it won't leave until there
is amity and amour
And when you go through it again
with the experience in hand
and expect the day as it comes
hoping it won't be a misery.

Silent Thoughts
by Mayar Akash

A Stranger just walked in
out of presence into nature
a stranger so new yet so cute
a glimpse a sigh pressure unloads
the mind and the heart

A stranger yet to be discovered
a stranger yet to be known
and yet the message is unbroken
a broken voice, low as the shallow stream
that runs through the air
a sight for sore eyes

A moment
of music a moment of eagerness
ebbs of sorrow memories flow out
a moment no longer than eddy of thoughts
that creeps into mind
when it then disappears without a sigh.

A stranger so new yet the effect
yet the thought
thus the image crawling into a silent image.
To amend the embroiled distaste and elaborate the thinking.

Standing In The Middle
by Mayar Akash

Falling in love is easily done
recovering after breaking up is hard to follow
Courage is needed throughout
the emotional process of love
Kissing, hugging, sharing feelings
and words is fun in doing so

But when something stands in the middle
the feelings become intense
but the heartaches slows you down
you want to cry
but tears don't emerge from your eyes

Only to turn into grinders
and start grinding your heart inside
till it finishes you in doing so

But true love never dies
the joy and the happiness sometimes
leads to sorrow
Only to find that love has disappeared
into thin air like dust
But a wall stands in the middle
only to save a little of our love
which tried to disappear from each other.

Adversity
by Tamanna Parveen

They thought virginity in innocence
how they forgot about pure soul
born to the earth
I was slipping back into that
parallel world
where visions were bad and
smells were toxic
a place where words were fake and
promise a joke
hearts would break and
justice was a myth
so don't lie to me
because they robbed my smile
broke my soul
then they told me
don't let a bad day set your course
Justify your life and
determine your outcome.
adversity …
I think I found my purpose.

Unleash My Pain
by Mayar Akash

I'm in love and I'm in love with you
I've tried to tell you
I've approached you many times
I've rehearsed the things that
I want to say to you a millionth time
yet every time I see you I fall apart
drown in what I want to say.

Things that I want to say to you are locked up inside
and its giving me pain.

I've seen you many times & I'm stuck on you
I know you've noticed me
and I Know you know because you give space
and every time I drown.

Please help me unleash my pain,

save me from drowning
say "hello" or "Hi" and "what's on your mind";
"let's talk about it".

Squeeze me
by Mayar Akash

I want to chain you
to my heart and
I want you to;

Squeeze me, tease me
do anything you want
but hurt me

Kiss me, hug me
do me like you want to
over every part of my body

Touch me, feel me
rub your body all over mine
give my mind ecstasy

Love me, hold me
don't let me free
until I come, to you.

Seize It
by Mayar Akash

If something you want
you find it

don't hesitate
secure it

If someone you want
comes by you

don't wait
otherwise it will be too late

act on your impulse
on the things you desire

otherwise you will lose them
another chance might be an eternity away.

On Your Own
by Mayar Akash

I've tried to do things and business
I've looked for opportunity
I looked for help
looked for support
looked for guidance
looked for chances
but no one wants to give or help
not for free -

People want something for nothing
con you into or con you out

The Dew Of Meteorology
by Nirmal Kaur

The glistening blitz of back to Russia with love.
 I turned back to remember the revolutionary forlorn,
territorial,
kinship did fade into oblivion
as indeed there was none to buy
or leave was a good escape.

Finally racing through the departure lounge
had made it to Robin Hood Gardens.
And managed to access the Mulberry dew.

There was a national crisis on.
It was very melodramatic.
And not provocative at all
after passing the brush off door.
And at the point of access to reality.
I was amidst a reality that really exists
it's a borough.

It's called Tower Hamlets
and after passing the torrential, rains and mildew.
There was a remembrance
our borough Tower Hamlets
has a mayor of its own.

Dark Room
by Mayar Akash

Until I got married
I was locked up in a cold
and dark lonely room

Nothing set me free
I did not even try
even though
I was aware of the bright world

Now that I have been freed
from my isolation
my spirit has come to life.

Bad Byes
by Mayar Akash

When you have to part
without a just reason
there's no such thing as a good bye.

A good bye is a good bye
all's well and all the best
but in circumstances
of breaking apart
there's no good byes.

There's nothing good about breaking apart
all the heartaches,
sadness,
sorrow and guilt
all the bad feelings and bits dwell
so I say so long and a very bad bye.

On Air
by Mayar Akash

The effect you had on me
elated, buzzing,
high in ecstasy,
walking on air

what can I say
my tongues tied
and I'm lost for word
all I can do is stare.

While my head was
stuck in the clouds
and I was walking on air

You in my mind
nothing else I could find
my feelings were very unkind
to my heart, my mind and my soul

I was high on you
there was nothing
nobody could do
except you.

Fixated
by Mayar Akash

When I am in love
my mind shuts everything out
except you

I'm so hooked on you
that I am umbilically linked to you
and I can't let anybody else in

You have become the view
when my eyes are open
and you are the eternal light
when I close my eyes.

I've got you in me
even before we made contact

You have become
a part of my soul and
under control from within

I can't see eye to eye or
think rationally

All I know is
that I'm fixated on you

A Droplet Amongst Thousands
by Julie Archbold

Turned to stone
The river once young and yielding
Turns cold

Its' clearness shadowed by a murky turbulence
At the bed
At the heart

One droplet amongst thousands
Flows through
Down my cheek
Scarred by the deep

Its' passage slow and steady
Meandering around the bank
Tickling the crease of my nose

Jumping over each eddy, each ripple
Its' path relentless
And salty on my mouth

What Is Your Colour?
by Mayar Akash

What is the colour of your soul?
that is the colour of mine.

What is the colour of your blood?
that is the colour of mine.

What is the colour of your mind?
that is the colour of mine.

What is the colour of your pain?
that is the colour of mine.

What is the colour of your tears?
that is the colour of mine.

What is the colour of your life?
that is the colour of mine.

What is the colour of your thoughts?
that is the colour of mine.

What is the colour of your desires?
that is the colour of mine.

What is the colour of your love?
that is the colour of mine.

What is the colour of your dreams?
that is the colour of mine.

What is the colour of your hate?
that is the colour of mine.

What is the colour of your sorrow?
that is the colour of mine.

What is the colour of your knowledge?
that is the colour of mine.

How is it that you are special?
Then, I.

Ripple
by Mayar Akash

Ripples in the sea
that is what we are

flow away with me
to another shore

Where we can flow
in and out together

flowing in and out
one ocean to another

One ripple to another
when ripples turn into waves
O oh

How can we escape
this love we have for each other
O oh.

one ripple to another
a ripple to a wave
o oh

Deshi Girl
by Mayar Akash

My deshi girl
and I want you so

She's my deshi girl
you are my ocean pearl

My deshi girl
I want to be in your world

I want to share your world
oh my deshi girl

Love you and be with you
my brown eyed deshi girl

your black hair makes me curl
Oh my brown skinned deshi girl

My deshi girl
and I want you so

In Life
by Mayar Akash

You come first,
protect yourself,
believe in yourself
love yourself,
trust yourself,
help yourself
Look after yourself,
keep judgments to yourself

help yourself to help others
don't make yourself vulnerable

take it easy, be patient, give time, be fair
be compassionate, share

Don't do anything to others,
that you wouldn't like it done to you.

Not to have sex before marriage,
Not to fornicate
not to cause pain,
not to cause suffering
not to gossip,
not to hurt anybody
not to deprive anybody of food

You have to earn respect
think before you do anything
you have to be courteous
make others happy
happiness is food of life
work hard now and play later.
take advantages of opportunities
give opportunities.

My Little Soul
by Julie Archbold

A passion for this Earth I feel
Compassion which is oh so real
My blood flows through Earth's lava veins
My tears reflected in her rains

The winds which circulate the Earth
Breathe in and out of me from birth
The cyclic rhythms of her tides
Are matched by how I feel inside

Yet most remarkable of all
Open your heart to hear the call
The essence which I know is me
Is here in everything I see

Believe
by Mayar Akash

That all plants & tree of all kind
filters the earth and soil

Trees and plants filter out a lot of greens
flowers filter out all the colours of the spectrum

all the fruits and berries filter all the colours too.

All the vegetables filter out everything too

I believe green is the colour of life, Soul.

Shoes
by Mayar Akash

Black velvet shoes
black suede shoes

Black velvet and suede shoes
they give me the woos
sizzle my thoughts
spark my moods

Black velvet and suede shoes
oh, baby I want you
velvet and suede shoes
making me crazy.

Black velvet and suede shoes
make my soul oooooooh
oh, my god I want you

My Side Of The Story
by Mayar Akash

The time came,
the moment sprung from above and I knew it.
When all the heart aches begin and
our story ends or is it yours.
My love for you is still strong I love you and you know it,
deep down inside you know it too if you wanted to.

My heart aches,
I feel hurt,
I see hurt,
I see you and I know it,
it's you

I hope not because of what's been done and said, beheld.
Thinking of what has been the past
.
I know it,
I cry in vain I find no reasons.
I try to beget the reason by sinking my thoughts in my tears.
Where I saw them appear,
I saw no one
I only saw predictions and compromise being fought where it
has been predicament.

I try to accuse myself over and over again thus, no.
I'm not alone you are the other side of this story
I hide the truth,
I find no truth,
I find no solution,
I plea for forgiveness.

Atomise this error forever and
 liquidise the heartaches into misty water.
I make myself believe,

I alone am the guilty shadow thus, no.
You say forgive,
forget and try,
I ask why?

You make no sigh, you stay low, you know the limit
no answer yet to mend, tit for tat second to none
ready or not I want another chance
I know you used me in many ways it's hard to sling away.

Now you had enough you turn your back away and say "goodbye".
I feel hate,
been a fool played around explored by a stranger.
I try hard,
I feel alone and stranded amongst the corpses of our memories.
Yet again I ask forgiveness as I can't let go,
you give me a unpleasant look.

I gained the roughness of your pleasure,
it's my sacrifice to you
In time I too may forget yet may not forgive for what I endured.
I won't cast my anger or disguise my love for you,
my love is rooted in my heart and in our cindered remains;
I've laid a wreath of roses
to remember you in my side of the story.

Corners Of My Mind
by Mayar Akash

Need and acceptance
Approval and love

I need you, I accept you
I approve of you, I love you

I want to be needed
I need to be accepted
I need to be approved
I need to be loved

The four corners of my mind.

The Daffodil
by Mathew Whiting

As Achilles treads February's
dreary pasture
Aching heels over dormant Earth

The infant stirs within.
Bursting through the Earth
with starlight fire

Like Persephone breaking the
bonds of hades.
Glowing in the mist of the morning's
sun kissed dew,

Perfect in Heavens design,
Marriage of terrestrial and celestial
Radiant as the warmth of the heart,
And full of the promise of
Apollo's fiery chariot

Resplendent with the rays
of the lion's golden mane.
And shining like my love for you,
Daffodil.

If Love Means
by Mayar Akash

If falling in love means
heartaches and sleepless nights

If falling in love means
isolation and loneliness

If falling in love means
insecurity and pain

If falling in love means
losing your faith and self esteem

if falling in love means
you lose, lose yourself

If falling in love means
you lose your mind, your love,

If falling love means
losing the will to live and your world.

Then think again.

Novelty-ness
by Mayar Akash

Novelty
Wares out
Novelty runs out

Novelty of the bride
novelty of the wife
the freshness
the newness
the guest-ness

the wonder,
the surprise
the discovery
the mind

becomes
use-to-ness
seen
familiar-ness
and residence-ness

The concentration and tolerance
patients and understanding
gets reduced
limited
overstretched

Let Go
by Mayar Akash

The only way out of heartaches
is to let go of everything

Focus on one thing
never let it out of sight
it's the only thing you need to
hold dear and tight
no matter what
It's the one thing worth your fight
and that's, you.

Work hard, work harder
don't give too much else
don't give time to anyone
focus on yourself.

don't let anyone in
don't give anything out
you got to be strong
you got to be hard as rock.

Focus hard
drive yourself harder
make your pains work
drive away your heartaches
and never drop your guards
always be busy never stop
never stop to think of the past.

Princess Diana
by Mayar Akash

Your death
- for what you stood for
what you did in the public eyes -

I, like others grew up with you every day of our lives;
Like the northern star,

You made an impact in all our lives
you sparkled when the royal's faltered

You left behind those sparkles that warmed our hearts
your presence kept us in touch with the monarchy

You were the royal inspiration that captivated our lives
and you left the sparkle locked in our eyes and in our thoughts

For your deeds and for your worth
you've paid the highest price.

Your death, gives birth to "Princess Diana",
You will live on in our hearts,

Though you're up in heaven, you'll never be far
further then the northern star;

as you've shown in our lives and never want you to dim
So therefore I rename the northern star after you.

The "Princess Diana" in memory of you and what you have given to me and the people of this world; warmth, human touch and hope.

Believing
by Rashma Mehta

Believing means you can choose what,
when and how to do things
Believing means doors open
Believing allows you to see the light
Believing is unique

Believing means new ideas
Believing means new opportunities
Believing means new challenges
Believing means no one stands in your way

Believing means chasing dreams
Believing means opening new dreams
Believing means a new chapter
Believing means new beginnings

Use To Think
by Mayar Akash

I use to think everybody was nice
I use to think everybody was kind
I wanted to believe that everybody was nice and kind

I use to think everybody would be nice to me
I use to think everybody would be kind to me
I use to think everybody be like my mum and dad
I use to think everybody would be that mother and father figure
I use to think everybody
I use to think everybody

Since my minds been taken,
bewitched and meddled with
now it knows.

Reality has its stink.

My Bewildered Mind
by Mayar Akash

Though I try hard
very hard and yet
I can't think straight

Having come this far
with commitments, strain
pain, anger and frustration
it feels as if I've never journeyed

As I am none the wiser
as I just remember
nothing of the past
but the present that I feel I'm locked in.

Upbringing
by Mayar Akash

My upbringing set me up to;

believe that everything in life
will be just fine

Everyone will look after me
keep an eye on my well being

Protect me from the bad
and direct me to my goals

Guide me in a rewarding path
and provide opportunities for me to prosper.

Freedom
by Mayar Akash

What is freedom?
Here is how I look at freedom.

I close my eyes and imagine
looking into the distance
all that I see is the horizon
with the vastness of space.

The view in front of me
clear as far as the eyes can see
nothing holding me, no weight on me
free to do what I please.

I'm free in the vastness of space
yet poses me a dilemma,

I can run around in circles
laugh, scream,
shout, jump up and down
but get nowhere, or.

Look ahead into the vastness
have the horizon in sight;
mark a point and set my goal
and work towards it or them.

The vastness holds my goals
my goals are my destiny
and the choice I make is my,
"Freedom".

Glastonbury Chalice
by Mathew Whiting

Glastonbury Chalice
You can't have a chalice
in Glastonbury
It would let the people free

you can't have a chalice
in Glastonbury
it would cause too much unity

What's going on in Babylon system
keep the people down
you can see it happening
rise and look around

you can't have a chalice
in Glastonbury
they won't let you smoke the
pipes of peace.

You can't have chalice
in Glastonbury
what would it release?

Mt pain? my stress?
my deep unrest
why the ignorant system
destroying the herb god blessed!
though through the torment the sorrows
ans the woes
they can't stop herb
it just grows and grows

The Weight Of Your Stare
by Mayar Akash

The weight of your stare
and the weight of my stare
the sparks that flared
like the sparks of a welder.

The weight of the stares
have welded my mind
and my heart together
with the thought of us
and what we could have been.

Heart Watering
by Mayar Akash

Good looking girls
gorgeous girls
heart watering stunners
all looks and flare

One look and my heart does a runner
one thought and my mind halts

beautiful babes
living under parents wallet
blossoming to full bloom
under daddy's cares

Where looks comes first
then everything follows
when what people think dictates;
while the house struggles to be comfortable.

Hold Your Tears
by Mayar Akash

Hold your tears
don't cry

Don't cry
hold your tears

Don't cry
save your tears

don't make your tears cheap
save your tears for the day
that you wan
t to cry but tears don't come.

Hold your tears
don't drop them away for me or anyone
don't let it out.

Grow Out Of Your Childhood
by Mayar Akash

Don't grow up,
don't rush to grow
don't grow up quick
don't hurry
let time take you there;
and it does, time never fails.

Everybody gets all the chance
to be older, grow old and get older;

but you only get a starting chance
only one chance to be a child, young, youthful;

don't be an adult
when you need to
be a child,
to grow out of your childhood.

Being Strong Enough
by Rashma Mehta (Lyrics)

Being strong enough to face my past.
Being strong enough to face my troubles.
Being strong enough to face my fears.
Being strong enough to face the real emotions I feel.

Being strong enough to face what you can't
Being strong enough to face what you can't
Being strong enough to face what you can't
Being strong enough to face what you can't

Being strong enough to face reality.
Being strong enough to take control.
Being strong enough to face the hurt you feel.
Being strong enough to face the heartache you feel.

Being strong enough to face what you can't
Being strong enough to face what you can't
Being strong enough to face what you can't
Being strong enough to face what you can't

Being strong enough to face your enemy.
Being strong enough to face the outside world.
Being strong enough to face your experiences.
Face what you can't by being strong enough.

On Top Of Me
by Mayar Akash

I haven't been practicing my religion
and every day things are and have piled on me
emotions,
goals,
directions,
feelings,
thoughts,
people,
attitude have all got on top of me.

My life is full of doubt
my thoughts have become dense
my future looks like a lousy rainy winters day.

I've lost my peace and tranquility
I feel vulnerable and feel insecure
I'm too worked up and frustrated and confused.

I want to cry out and say
what's happening to me
what is happening to my life
why can't I find peace in my life

I need some peace
I can't find peace
why can't I find peace
but I don't ask
because people will try to show me god.

Why Special Then
by Mayar Akash

Why was then so special -
that prophets reigned
religions came and formed
miracles happened and took place

what was so special then that isn't special now.

days are still days
and night are still nights
people are people,
animals are animals
and the earth is still the earth

so why was then so accepted as
the religion of today remains then in time.

Conmen's Victims
by Mayar Akash

Like a conmen's victim, we get conned

Conmen make us believe
that nothing is worth something
and something is worth everything

They make us believe
what we cannot see and make what we see
the biggest thing we will ever see.

The conmen will sell you "nothing" for something
and something for everything;
and he'll make you believe
that you have bought the best thing ever.

Point In Life
by Mayar Akash

I've come to a point in life
where I pressed hard
I just can't seem to find a way through
I'm faltering and flustered, turned out
all commitment are burning me out

I want to lighten my load
but again, I don't want to lose my own
I want to lighten my
responsibilities
but I don't want to run away
from the duties
I've taken on

Branded By A Kick
by Julie Archbold

Oh, a whopping great horse was he
The one that caused injury to me

At eighteen hands high
Muscled, yet thin
That beast kicked a great hole in my shin

I writhed, yelled and screamed in a dance
But that steed, gave me not a glance

So, here I must lay
To dream of the day

I'm out of the plaster
Never will I be that horses' master

Who Are You To Judge
by Mayar Akash

My faith,
my belief,
my submission,
my devotion
is connected direct to divinity.

Who are you to judge me?
Divinity will judge me

Who gave you the authority to judge me?
It is between me and my Divinity

Who judges you?
So do not judge me -
assumptions do you wrong

So think about yourself
before you even begin to contemplate
to judge me.
As you have already been judged.

Man And Woman
by Mayar Akash

Man and Woman
Woman and Man.

Purpose of the man
is to give life.

Purpose of the woman
is to bare life.

Fundamental principle of
man and woman is to bring about new life.

The only expectation of
man and woman is to become mother and father.

What makes man?
conception
witnessing
fathering

What makes woman?
Giving birth to a child makes a woman.
Child disconnecting from the umbilical cord makes a mother.

Nature
by Mayar Akash

Natures law
Food chain
Reproduction

Everything comes and goes
everything gives birth and then dies
everything multiplies and grows
then gives birth and then dies

Natures law
we humans do the same
we are born to die
we live to reproduce
we die to continue.

Eat My Words
by Mayar Akash

Before you came along
I use to hate little infants
rampaging in the house
messing everything up
and doing anything
climbing,
touching,
throwing,
pulling,
biting,
licking,
screaming,
crying and much more.

Now that your here
there is not much
I could do
but eat my own words
as you have shown me what you can do.

Steps of Blood
by Kalam Choudhury

O the children of Bongo
whenever the 8th of Falgun arrives
Your memory returns.
I remember how your bosoms
were riddled with bullets
as you stood for the mother tongue's honour
on that blood spilling day
The pitch covered avenues of Dhaka
were stained red with your own blood
that's why we remember you today with reverence.

O indomitable boy
you have taught us
how to stand against injustice
snubbing the red eye of autocracy
you created history
treading on that bloody historical map
we have snatched away the red sun of independence
but-
that independence is imperilled today
by the conspiracies of the national traitors.

O heroic soldiers-
whenever Ekush is due, preparation starts
for acting as ultra-revolution, like-
placing of floral wreaths at the alter-foot,
walking of bare-foot to the Shaheed Minar,
Observance of one minute silence
by standing up at seminars,
and dancing- singing sessions everywhere
this is merely cheating
for self publicity.
On this blood spilling day
I pray for the salvation of your souls.

Gorgeous Girl
by Mayar Akash

Gorgeous girl
you look good with curls
I can't help but stare...
oooooooh at your curves.

You look at me
as you walk on by
I say to myself
oh my god help me sigh,

The thought of you
makes my mind bumper car ride
my heart melt
like strawberries make mouth water

you make my mind lose control
my heart thunder
and put a glow on my soul
because your gorgeous! girl.

Bus Job
by Mayar Akash

It's a big red thing
        and the wheels go round and round…
How much?
How far?
at what price?

        Start stop people come on board and then get off
but hate the job
bus driver job
yet like driving
the VA Volvo
but not the Route masters
        that leaves you jittery that needs to be slept off;
or the Titans

        King of the road, traffic jam, or bumper to bumper
        whoaaaw!, watch the cyclists scissor in and out in front
        and hate being on the spares list
hate working seven days on the trot.

        The big red bus job what a meander of life on wheel.

Frack E.U
by Mathew Whiting

The City looms, dull and drab
sat on the earth, a concrete scab
and underneath it sorely festers
and of its fate, you don't want to Jester.

For underneath the leader's mirth
is that rumour of Satanic birth?
Have the seeds of fate been sown?
Is he set to rule the beast called Rome?

Your Stare
by Mayar Akash

The weight of your stare
so intense
it penetrated deep down within me

I intended, to find out,
what was there?

Now that we, did not happen.
All I do now, is wonder.

Where we could have been?

One Of My Wonders
by Mayar Akash

I find myself wondering

It seems funny
I wonder
sitting on the loo
all on my own
no one there
just myself and
the natures call.

What a funny place?
all to myself
it is a funny place
it is a haven
where your inner
peace finds a presence.

Tell A Lie
by Mayar Akash

I realised, somewhat painfully
that I can't seem to lie
that I can't tell a lie
convincingly to save my life

I can't also trust people
I suspect all
A conspiracy
exploitation
boy, I must be paranoid

If I am,
I am,
I have been there and
it is no doing of mine.

Can't Forget The Weight
by Mayar Akash

I can't forget the weight of your stare
I can't stop my own haunting me.

I wanted you
and I know from your stare you wanted me

Only now
it hits me
it hits me hard
it hits me badly deep down in my guts

How badly we wanted each other
How sad it is that we didn't

The weight of your stare dwells in me
is has sunk into me

Its only now
I can imagine
how far we could have gone
now I know I could have taken it far

That is what haunts me
is the fact that were we could have taken it.

Mourn
by Mayar Akash

Let me mourn my loss
on my own
no matter the odds
Leave me be,
alone
so that I could see
what I've inherited,
who I've succeeded
why was I the chosen one
am I the only one
in this time of destiny

Fruits of Independence
by Kalam Choudhury

The loos of life that started
at the mango garden of Polashi
Due to Mirjazar's betrayal,
continues to date.

The same cause acted behind the brutal
killings at Jallianwalabagh and Chittagong
because the traits of oppressors and oppression
have not after hundreds of years altered.

The independence that the valiant boys have snatched
at the cost of a sea of blood,
Its fruits are still not enjoyed by the people of Bengal;
screams for food and clothes can be heard
even today in the sky and wind of Bengal.

Re-Gain
by Mayar Akash

Joi Bangla!
Our sonar Bangla
Joi to the people
joyous to their might
Joi to their happiness
tears for their pain
Praise to the dead
praise to their wounds
Praise them high
Praise the low
Praise them with a bit of heart and soul.

Joi Bangla
Our sonar Bangla
Enriched with the finest beauty

A world of its own
to be discovered
The wisdom which lies
untouched
Yet to reborn
yet to gain
and yet it shall rise again.

My April Love
by Mayar Akash

In spring,
I had change of heart
the sensation was so new,
yet few
my existence ripped apart
my soul,
my heart and
my mind knew.

Like the season
my feelings grew
until they blossomed
my April love
was in bloom.

My Valentine
by Mayar Akash

You are my valentine
knowing you is a crime
every time I see you

I chime
I can't say much
but, I try to mine

I know this for sure
I would like you
to be mine.

Identity
by Rashma Mehta

Identity is unique
Identity is true
Identity is power
Identity is within us

Identity is real
Identity is forever
Identity is who we are
Identity is different

Identity is part of us
Identity is deep
Identity is reality

Out of Touch
by Mayar Akash

Faith out of touch
no one to turn to confidently
and ask for a positive response

A one soul battle
time is holding back the answer
a truthful moment
arises almost each and everyday

While I lay here in my bed
my mind and soul is elsewhere
I'm wondering, how they are
What they're doing?

Being out of touch
Hurts like a paper cut.

Soul Cry
by Mayar Akash

You didn't make me cry
you made my soul cry
I heard my soul let it all go and the cries
Cried the agony
Anxiety and its bewilderness

While you can see what's going on
but, can't understand
Why it's happening the way it has
I'm all torn on the outside
soul cries inside.

Windmills
by Mayar Akash

My love for you is more than words
More than expressing and showing
My love for you is larger than life.

If I can show you my love
You will never see the end
If I can show you in windmills with my arms
Only death will stop it in your sight.

Love for you is immortal, so remember it.
Love me or hate me, you are my limb
A part of me, you possess my soul, so try and get rid of it
If you can succeed and forget – I will try to.

Witch Love
by Lora Ashman

Stir the day
stir the night
yes, beware of me
beware of me
your dearest enemy
from the south
from the north
or even east or west
watch out
here I come
the witch from Halloween.

Photo Gallery

Introducing
Penny Authors

"Championing the spirits within"

Zainab Khan

Paul Harvey

Mayar Akash

Rebekah Vaughan

Isaac Harvey

Mathew Whiting

Liam Newton

Prof. Md Nurul Huque

Julie Archbold

Kalam Choudhury

Akik Miah

Lora Ashman

Ellis Dixon-King

Rabia Mehmood

Nirmal Kaur

Tamanna Parveen

Rashma Mehta

"Spirits Championed"

For more information or if you would like to submit your work for inclusion, email: pennyauthers@yahoo.co.uk.